Undertaking the American Dream

Carmine Dandrea

FootHills Publishing

ACKNOWLEDGEMENTS

Counting Out My Growth In Deaths, *Plaintiff*, Spring, 1971
A Karate Expert Kills A Car, *Transition*, Spring, 1971
The 1st Of November, *Prize Poems Of Nfsps*, 1971
Sunrise In Chicago, *Blossom Review*, 1991
Alone In The House, *Prize Poems Of The Nfsps*
The Man From Yesterday, *Moravian Fantasy*, 1977
A Trinity For Maladjustment, *Touching Me, Touching You*
A Report From The Clinic, *Ego Flights*
I Love You, Minnie Wantaugh, In The A.& P., *Moravian Fantasy*
A Dead Horse In The Supermarket, *Michigan Magazine*, 1983
Waiting For The Third Wave In, *Prize Poems Of The Nfsps*
Rescue By Helicopter, *Husson Review*
The Universe Of Death, *Prize Poems Of The Nfsps*
An Elegy In Spring, *Elmira Review*
A Fable Of Flies, *Blossom Review*, 1992
The Blue Sky Motel, *Ego Flights*
Dreamland And Charles Bukowski, *Ego Flights*
Melville, *Prize Poems Of The Nfsps*
Estrangement, *Blossom Review*, 1994
M. Del Papa, *Blossom Review*, 1997
On The Eve Of The Gunfighter's Death, *Moravian Fantasy*
The Will That In The Sunset Finds Release, *Prize Poems*,Nfsps
A Dirge For The Dead Anatoly, *Blossom Review*, 1993
Sutra For Rama Singh, *Albion, Journal Of British Studies*
The Needled Husband, *Blossom Review*, 1991
Mr.Gupta, Mr.Li, *New Jersey Poetry Society*, 2007
In The Madras Market, *Blossom Review*, 1997,
Everyone Loved Fala, *Elmira Review*
Jumping Off The Eiffel Tower, *Touching Me, Touching You*

Cover photo montage by Carmine Dandrea

ISBN: 978-0-941053-88-4
FootHills Publishing
P.O. Box 68
Kanona, NY 14856
www.foothillspublishing.com

To Nancy who puts up with my poems
with love, critiques and courage

TABLE OF CONTENTS

COUNTING OUT MY GROWTH IN DEATHS

This sun-filled Sunday morning
when I woke,
I knew that you would not;
I knew that you had gone,
and that your eyes
were closed to Sundays
and to sun.

All my life
I have counted out my growth
in deaths
until they have become
the total of my time
as every stone
that makes a cairn
becomes a marker of the spot;
and your death, Grandfather,
is only one
among the many deaths
I register;
but how special to my growth
it is, I think I know.

At ninety years, your mind alive
to Sundays and to sun,
you simply fell asleep at five—
a quiet afternoon of naps—
and died. No pain we knew of
crossed you in that hour.
Of course, you were alone,
and that was fitting too.
The family had gone home
and left the dream you had
to you .

Who could have known,
although we were aware
at ninety every moment spins
a pinwheel in the sky,

and every arrow spun
is ever pointed straight.
Death smiles, sweet and sure
as lovers do in summer sun,
each time you close your eyes.

With you, another part of time
that calibrates my growth
and scales love has gone.
The sun of yesterday
will not be here tomorrow.
The sun, however, rises
as perhaps I do.
But you, old dial, stand still
the farthest measure of my hour.

I have counted out my growth
in deaths,
and yours is shortening
my life's shadow.
My growth slows
with fainter, thinner line
to mark my moments
in creative light.
The sun at noon is nude,
and so am I.

A KARATE EXPERT KILLS A CAR

He must have given it
at least one quick chop,
the car, maybe a buick,
more likely a fast ford
fending its way forward
with its tires leaving,
ultimately, in the skid
and swerve, a long streak
like some malicious tongue
lying out on the highway;
one brick-breaking slap
with the hard edge of his hand.

As his breaking bike broke
under the unequal forces
of a bike-hits-car collision,
he must have hieed once,
dealing the right front fender
a back blow to the light.

No stance around
could have dented
that approaching destiny:
head-over-handlebars;
legs splitting the air
like some peculiar shears
snipping at sunlight;
the broken bike spinning
its little eternities.

Over the flat hood
flying like sixty,
Hell's Angel, heavenbent.

THE 1ST OF NOVEMBER

That roofer's ladder leaning
up against my neighbor's house
points out the way:
the sky is gray
but for a strip of blue
that shows it still is day;
the air is slick as water.
I should do something with this day.
My son and daughter
are out somewhere at play.
I know that I must stay.
Were I to go,
what would I leave behind
except a somewhat troubled mind;
the simple truth that springtime ever comes;
a bed of dead chrysanthemums;
a book of poems that I have marked;
love left howling in the dark.
One thing I know
were I to go,
it must be with this coming snow
and must demand a change of will.
All else would be a lie,
the very notion of November to deny.
Yet, his ladder is pointing still
to that strip of blue beyond the hill.

THE IMAGE IN THE MIRROR

Night's anesthesia
dulls the waiting room;
my sister rests,
curled in a ball;
my brother startles in sleep
and wrestles an ancient guilt;
but the old man lies awake,
his eyes, frantic glows
in the darkened room.
I stroke his cold iron hair
with a trembling hand.
He is as tense as a question.

The scene is marked
with sentiment:
the falling rain,
the gray November day,
the lost son
driving through the night;
the mother—my mother—
wild-eyed with wonder
mixed with fear.

There is no sunrise
to cut the dawn asunder,
to say NO
to the terrible angel
who comes with steady step
to the threshold
of something new.
Not even the stones
dare say NO.

She dies, and I,
deadheaded among those
who come to funeral thought
in frivolous talk,
move through circles of regret,
move among

dry morsels of remorse;
yet, somehow,
through these commonplace events,
I move and stumble
into the realm of love.

She stands apart
from the event, apart
from the breathless object
that remains.

On this November day,
she moves beyond dimension
into me
as rays of warming sunlight must
to permeate the coldest stones.

Her universe expands my memory
to hold the whole that's real:
the parted seal
of eye and lid,
the song of voice,
the violet of breath, the flush on cheek
and hand and lip.

And so, she IS
until such memory fails
which is her death and mine.
We live again refreshed
when someone catches
at the latch of love
to hold the freshened image,
corporeal and new.
Failing this,
we fall to chaos
when the mirror
loses light.

SUNRISE IN CHICAGO

at the trial of John Wayne Gacy

The mothers on their benches roll;
their faces are the front pages
of tomorrow's newspapers.
It is slippery
on the courtroom floor;
all the bodies have been rolled in
in their plastic bags,
zipped up tight
and leaking the bad news
to the defense attorneys.

The eyes of the spectators,
more than any before
in this Federal Building's
chamber of horrors,
strain like seed spots
of flowers strain, forward
into the arms of the wind.

Everyone fears the justice
of the sanitarium:
the lugubrious lawyers
fretting at the bar;
the conflicting reports
of the mental landscape,
each taking wing
toward Paradise;
the series of shocks
working the Purgatorial animal
toward the pictures
of this world;
then, the final release
after 33 steps,
admitting Behemoth
into the pleasures
of the parlor.

At the last moment
before grace comes,

Gacy raises his round head,
lifts his round face
and chuckles softly
at the film stills
of Buchenwald,
coming alive
in the prosecutor's mouth.

The mothers are off their benches
and licking the dust
on the courtroom floor;
The fear in the room
is the fear of old Jews,
lining up for the ovens.

Again and again the tedium
of justice
seems destined to lie
in a footnote to Freud.

One wants to scream out
at darkness;
to rip off the blindfold
and tip up the scales;
to give vision to blindness;
to deflect human error
in the making of madness.

After two hours
of imaging hell,
of nightmaring
the release of Behemoth
into the darkening day,
the mothers are standing
in sunrise;
the dead boys
are rising to rainbows;.
It is resurrection
and Judgment Day in Chicago.

ALONE IN THE HOUSE

Alone in the house
with my head stuffed up
and my throat a Sahara,
after the children
have left for school
and the ghost of my wife
is off to work
in the flesh,
I wander through rooms
that have become
mirrors of myself,
cold and hard, without reflection.

I avoid the bedroom
completely
where the devil
of my old self
sits brooding on the bed
with the shades drawn.

And the morning
folds into afternoon
like a butcher's paper
around my red soul—
fold upon fold
of falling sunlight
through the windows
with the creases of shadows
as time becomes
the limits of light.

Then, as the afternoon ends
and the others return,
the walls cave in
with the weight of love,
the windows crack
with the pressure of light;
and I am joined
to myself again.

AN ELEGY IN SPRING

The springtime starkness
of these orchards seems
a thrust of winter at the heart,
yet in a single day
the bud will burst;
the sun and rain will start
each blossom—apple, cherry, pear—
on its journey from the inner life
into the outer air
to bloom at tip and fall;
to search the warming earth;
to bury whiteness from the tall
uncompromising shadows
of these springtime trees.

I could find myself at ease
with such a progress in my mind,
and it would please me to retell
the ancient comfort that the blind
poet spread upon the Grecian seas
with all the healing fingers of the Dawn;
but that the orchard starkness still remains
upon the prism of my eye;
but that the sharp, chill branches in my heart
still scratch the edges of the sky;
but that the blossom, even though
it comes each year, each year must go.

RISING AFTER MIDNIGHT

Rising after midnight
from the bed of my desire,
giving thought to her waiting
with an old patience
for my arrival,
I knew I could no longer give
what she desired;
yet I wanted to go to her
with a clod of dirt in my mouth,
showing I had resurrected all
higher than before, newer;
that all would be right again;
that she had not surrendered
all she was vainly,
merely for my pleasure;
that I understood, knew
and responded to her need,
would give what women want
at such times—love.
Only a word whispered in my ear,
the meaning gone now
like children are gone,
leaving with unstoppable birthdays.
Anything else would be contrition;
in all a lie, no more.
But I knew that I would go again,
dragging my spirit to her,
knowing that she knew, too,
pretending it would rise
like Lazarus restored,
a small chance of faith.
She wanted it so, loving a lie,
and I, lying love, both false
because we knew no way out.

THE MAN FROM YESTERDAY

This morning,
mourning fell into my brain,
a deadweight
to freight the shape of thought.

In the shaving mirror
I saw the stubble on my face;
behind me lay the rubble
of another time and place.

I said, "This man is dead."
I said, "His life bled out of him."
There in the mirror,
I found no fear in truth.
Here, outside the mirror,
I was absurd with fear.

Death has a curious way
of keeping lost men alive
well past their dying day:

although the hived head bumbles on
and the automaton stumbles
and puppets its way
through worlds of trees
as green as tomorrow's spring,
it still is yesterday.

The spirit sleeps its winter
like some furry thing
suspended in its breath
to keep all feeling at the depth
of zero in its bones,
as close to love and life
as cold and bloodless stones.

THE FLOWER MAN IS GONE: ELEGAIC STANZAS
for William Carlos Williams

Good-bye Billy Boy, gone now
    after your time spent
        at home in America.

You: bardic man, poet, Doc,
    entrepreneur of the busy word,
        the *mot just americain;*

deliverer of the flowery news
    in the natural republic of art,
        gone now to collect

your sweet deliverance in bloom
    in the poetic empyrean
        beyond the world's dream.

Son of a river—Paterson—
    become in time
        figure of a man;

image of a man in the water
    become in time
        persona of a river;

you put yourself clearly
    between Provencal Pound
        --pushing cantos on one side,

knowing no anemones in his florid heart,
    throwing no flowers
        to the wind—

and the inexorable weight of the idea-man
    --pressing hard from Hartford
        down to Keywest,

finding no flowers at all in America
    except as floral decorations:
        ideas for fruit—

you sought out a new America.,
          newer even than New Jersey,
                    clothed in a new language

purged of pretense and clean
          in the purity of idiom:
                    speaking American

like a native but in new rhythms
          yet unheard, unsung, un-un.
                    Hey, Billy Boy, where?

Your triple step stuck
          in the passionate mud
                    of America;

all flower here and weed there,
          deep-rooted with your mind
                    in the natural grain.

How is it that you brought home
          the Greek and Latin wreathes,
                    crowned upon your head,

despising them, the leaves unnatural,
          filled with hothouse heat,
                    the artificial artifice;

yet failed to find yourself in bloom,
          at heart's length, languishing
                    in utmost love?

You were the delicious, delirious
          dealer in damn words,
                    now pushing up daisies

and Queen Anne's Lace, lovingly,
          through the leafy lattice
                    of your flowered poems.

AN ESCAPE FROM THE INSTITUTION

I clap my hands to my ears
at the absolute silence,

the heavy sound of the white walls,
pressing the damp air.

Why I have come for this visit
is an unsolved mystery,

except that I know I must come
to keep the universe intact.

I have been told that the mind
can hold so much sound

before its link to the world
strains, bends, breaks.

I see only that her small hands
still hold flowers if they are given.

How then can her eyes be
such polished stones, gems,

reflecting the dull light
falling off walls,

as if her sight had frozen
solid, marble-hard?

Where, I wonder almost aloud,
is the cold Medusa that charms her?

At that bare sliver of sound, my breath,
she covers her ears

with her small cupped hands:
they are twin shells hiding

beneath flat stones, empty
even of sea sounds.

What had once lived in them
is gone elsewhere.

For an hour I become part of her wall,
as loud as the white paint,

as tactile as the painted wood,
as dead as its dull matte.

She moves through the room
as small fish move through water,

cutting the density until she becomes
lighter than air.

I know that when I leave,
she will be as knowing of me

as the white wall is,
as the loud silence is;

and I will return to the world,
knowing what walls know.

A TRINITY FOR MALADJUSTMENT

Even as a child, my ear
caught firm
between the finger
and grand thumb
of my majestic Grandmama,
I swayed to rhythms
running through my head
of ghostly dances,
tarantellas taught;
and I used to wet the bed;
so now I am afraid
to walk out in the shade
and scared to death
of lady fingers.
They make me catch my breath.

When on my spindly legs
and mostly sickly too,
I holidayed my way
through maladies
enough for children armies
on crusade
that lady Grandmama,
when fever struck
or germ or bite
or cruel strike
of others
to my hollow cheek,
would sweep me off,
come headache pain
or broken wrist
or simple sprain,
down Stowell Street Hill
to that dark house
where ancient *Zia* sat,
spreading in relentless fat.

Her hands, incredible and soft,
were wrinkled flesh
and boneless too.
They did their healing work
in tandem with a chain
of holy prayers
and olive oil dripped
in water mixed with salt
as she reported
on the human fault:
"Sono tutto, tutto
male occhio. Tutto."

No wonder, then, I jumped
to hearty health so soon.
Her fingers, Buddha-thick,
performed her art
upon my skin and bones.
Their loamy taste
still drips
upon my lips;
I bit old *Zia* once.
Thereafter, bloody mouth and all
were tightly taped
before she'd look or touch,
before she'd act or pray.

She loved her function;
oh, she knew it well:
manipulating nature
on a boy's slight frame.
How I would shiver there
like grass in rain.
Her eyes were opals,
shining in the room
like pearly clouds
that gleam through gloom
on rainy days.

Her rain fell in my heart,
extinguishing small flames.
Of course, I grew up
to maladjustment
and to queerness, too,
the unhappy product
of some magic art
I never knew,
involving three fat fingers
on an ancient lady's hand
mixed up with Grandmama and God,
all in the pearly dark,
until all three
were blended into one,
and Grandmama became
Almighty God and worse,
for he became my Grandmama.
As for the third,
old, wrinkled *Zia*
in her fatty folds,
what else for her
than spirit, ghost,
old metamorphosis:
the devil needs a human form.

HOW THE OLD MAN DIED

As B*abbo* was old and empty,
ninety, nearly floating
through the house,
we anchored him with love
loose enough to pin him down
and held him fast
with talk—gossip—
which he loved, and so,
held him awhile
against the fall of night.

Days he agreed to be
merely an old man broken
with remaining time
clutched in his wrinkled hands,
waiting for the relentless hour
when light would fail
and darkness shadow
all reflection
in his empty eyes.

But, as day ended
and the endless night came on,
he floated; arms suspended
at his sides, he stretched
back to yesterday.
We couldn't hold him then
with all our love;
none of our small talk
could rope him down,
and he would pick us off
one by one
with the whiplash
of his tongue—

stories as old as garden roots,
truths broken, half truths, lies,
traveling back before even he

had traveled over foreign sea
from one lifetime to another.
How he mixed his life
with the lives of others!
The great men he had heard about,
chaining the facts
of both his time and theirs,
until an Alexander
was his neighbor as a boy
in Tuscany;
a Titus really stood
beside his Gate at home;
and he conversed in Latin
with some Caesar still in Rome.

He would float high
and nothing we could do or say
could bring him down again
into the confines of the room
where ghostly figures fell
and rose up in the gloom.

And this went on for weeks,
for months, for years it seemed
while we worked out our hardships
in the world, and yet came home
each night to play his game
of broken truths and lies.

We played it well
and with a strength of heart
because we knew
that once his ghosts were gone,
our work at love was done.

We knew that he would fly
one solo more

out from the talky room
into the stiffening dark
where stars were Roman candles
going out at his approach;
and knew that we would do
what needed to be done—
what he had left for love—
to pick up his deflated soul
and lift his undefeated spirit up
after he had circled down
and landed finally
in the evening world.

A REPORT FROM THE CLINIC

She has always been a closet case:
when she was very young—
before the long process
of bleeding out her life began—
she was mind-locked,
she was wit-stitched
by an enormous hour
that has never ended.

Her Freudian father,
in a fit, nitwitted her,
locked her in a dark closet
beneath her mother's furs
which, by capricious malice,
rubbed her soft-downed face
like paws of bears
in woods at night.

She never quite made
the sunlight after that.
As a girl she held to trees,
letting their shade
grove her golden hair

At twenty-one she was a mouse
living in a dark burrow
and looking out at day
through smoked glass.

Now, as a woman, long in desire,
she anticipates the closet.
Love is a furred arm
brushing past her cheek,
and the bed is alive with bears.

EVERYTHING IS SPRINGTIME
AND GREAT BEAUTY

She comes to me
and puts her hand upon me in the night,
but it is day and I,
I am awake—no,
asleep under her hand.
And do I dream? Yes. No.
And do I cry out?

Mother, I wish I were born again
into the new day,
born into springtime and great beauty,
born into the new suit you bought for me
when I was nine, born to be again,
with the confessions in my hands
at First Communion
in a time without time.

I wish there were priests again—
the old-time priests in golden robes,
in deep purple robes, in pure white robes,
in black-scarfed robes, chanting, chanting;
and nuns too, yes the nuns, again and again,
the high-starched nuns
in the great white wimples
and the taut black headdresses
that towered high as the rocks
where my horses run and mate in the sun.

I wish for the orange again, split three ways,
and for the red penny we put into the meter
and for the water from the red penny,
the clean, fresh water that ran
into my face, into my hands, into my heart,
cleaning, cleaning, as I ran into the sun
in my new suit with the communion
white in my mouth, unchewable,

sticking to the roof like a hot coal,
and the priest hurting me with his looks:
"Christ's gonna getcha now."

And the nuns, the nuns especially the big ones,
all clapping their hands for us kids to sit,
to rise, to stand, to kneel, to wait,
to fly, to live, to die.

Mother, Mother,
in the windy, nun-filled night, I wait
but you do not come.
Mother, I cannot stay,
Mother, I cannot breathe,
Mother, I cannot live here any longer.

In the windy center
of this world and another,
where horses run up mountains
to mate in the sun,
where is there a place for me?
Where can I hide, Mother?
Where can I go?
To what country, to what star,
to what room dressed in white
where the walls cannot hear,
where the walls cannot speak,
where the walls cannot question,
and never, never give any answers?

Mother, Mother
the nuns are coming out of the walls,
out of the ceilings,
out of the deep basements of my mind;
and the priests are coming too;
and I do not know where to go,
why I am here, what to do.

There are horses falling out of the sky,
spotted horses, falling,
and the sky is falling too,
falls upon them as they lie
in all the green, green grass
that's browned out now,
that's died for lack of water,
for lack of sun, for lack of sky,
for lack of sense,
for lack of—of—love.

JUNGLE

This room is like a small jungle,
smelling of the fake chatter
of make-believe monkeys
and holding its own nose
against the spoor of phony tigers
that roam the rain forests
in the southeast corner
by the big bay window.

If you are no Tarzan,
I am no Jane. Just
the lack of civilized response
bridges our two lives.

We swing through jungles
in this leafy room,
meeting each other
on purely physical vines;
and the only sound that's real
is the monkey chatter
of our souls,
flying through treetops.

FARM AUCTION

These German farmers,
Lutherans by trade,
slow-headed, thick-faced,
their hands
deep in cherry trees,
stand together
and watch their brother
sold out of the world of work.

Their lost hands fumble
through apple sorters,
berry baskets,
rusting Deeres.
If they are moved,
it is not
by apple blossoms in the air
nor by the disenchanted orchards
falling down
nor the discarded vines.
They are up to their elbows
in barrels of apples,
turning green into cash.

The worn halters,
the swingletrees
in dryrot majesty,
the bales of amiable hay,
go for pennies;
the tenant beds and stoves
for more or less the same;
bolt-rusted pulleys,
time-dried scythes,
stiff-necked yokes,
the cracked and strained
gee and haw
from the dead furrows
are sold by lots.

I, too, am caught
in the auctioneer's ear
for a fraction,
making hay
in the dead farm's face.

DREAMLAND AND CHARLES BUKOWSKI

Near the Golden Gate Bridge,
bearded, electrified,
Charles Bukowski
is having an apotheosis,
thinking himself
into Ginsberg and Ferlinghetti.

He is awake in Dreamland
with Mr. America,
superstripping in comics,
making California:

the brawling, the beer,
the bawling broads,
the exhibiting pose
with slack stomach,
shacked with straw,
colored Captain Marvel
in the deathless sun.

Before his spot freezes over,
I can see beneath the disguise,
beneath the dead afternoons,
a golden muscle of light
flex over the Pacific
and the hanging bridge:

some small chance of life
against the freezing time,
unnoticed in the clutter
of deadbeats and drunks,
of washed-out whores
and pious old guys
kissing walls.

And I spread on Bukowski
like salve over raw wounds.

MELVILLE

The god was marbleheaded in you
that pushed out the land's limits
and drew you, sculptured
like the molded waves
beyond the New York shore,
fetched once and for all
from under the grand melee
of your brother's furs and caps.

The will was wild that led you
from the upstate farms
that fed your double yearning
and from the broadening city's boom
to the Acushnet's decks;

and wilder still the will
that slipped you off
in the Marquesas
and later from Papeete's shores,
cruised out.

But the sharp bone that shaped
deep in your darkest mind
was honed then for the world,
the body, and the grave;
for the slicing cycles,
the merging circles
of heaven and earth;
for the mystic mandorla
holding in twin circumference
the opposites of life:

the great carved curve
in the marbled whale fluking
through your sounding mind
and moving into mine
is the penetrating god
that pulls blood into tides
in all men and drives
the tides of meaning
through our watered veins.

ESTRANGEMENT

You are a vast perimeter,
a far distant circumference,
touching the edges
of some unknown world—
a jungle, perhaps,
given your savage disposition.

Is there some way to reach you,
touch you, find out
your ready desires
without some Livingstone
or Stanley to explore
the hidden way
through your dark continent?
without some safari to trek across
your long lost tracks.

How can I contend with you
the wastelands of lost love
without an army
of exotic mercenaries
to force your impenetrable walls?

Why, just to talk with you
about the most mundane events—
the jungle heat, the splintered stones,
the long list of supplies to take along—
demands intercontinental cables
and stretches the imagination
beyond all jungles.

ON THE EVE OF THE GUNFIGHTER'S DEATH

He lies here, somewhere
between the falling sun,
smothered in haze,
and the coming rain,
an historical fact
in a black sombrero,
his image intact,
silver-spurred,
in the sights of my mind,
filling the landscape:

the cactus pinches the sky,
its spikes glint
like arrows in flight;
spotted horses whinny
up in the hills,
their hard hoofs
striking sparks
on the rims of rocks.

Everywhere is midnight
in the gunfighter's mind
and his mind is everywhere.
I know he has had Indian women
as spotted as ponies,
as long-legged as pintos
sprinting in grass.

Once, white stallions
worried them out of his tepee;
now, they sleep nude in his arms
under the buffalo grass.
I can smell the fragrance
of their bright nipples
in the dark air,
and I desire Indian women.

I hold the whole bone
of his skull in my mind,

dry as an old waterhole
sunk in the desert.
Through it I see
the dust rise in the street,
the sun glare without shadows,
the driving wind roll
the tumbleweed off,
and the six-gun shimmer
in the terrible heat.
Then, his sweat-soaked shirt
explodes in fountains of blood
through the fibers and dirt.

Driller ants march in thin columns
through his joints and his porous bones.
My cigarette burns,
sending up puffs of white smoke
to the Indian camp.

Sharp arrows fester
in my dark mind,
their shafts broken off,
their heads still on fire,
filled with Apaches
holding tight to my hair.

All this is a lie
where he lies, silent,
moldering well;
but I search the sky
for a sign
of Indian weather.

I let my left hand
swing low to my hip
where already the bone
is beginning to rot
under the butt of his gun,
and the midday sun
explodes into midnight.

UNDERTAKING THE AMERICAN DREAM
A report from the U.S.A., 1969

All through the dying day
we heave our breasts
against the Nightmare
resting on our chests;
all through the living night,
embalmed in dread delight,
we lie awake
and sweat out dreams
shrouded in our damp hands,
ready for the undertaking.

The Mafia Bangman lights his cigarette
from our burning fingertips,
remnants of the American Dream
now lying cold and wet
in the hard cement on the river floor.
There patriotic fishes
nibble off the toes
of our gone generation.

Whitman knew the democratic devil well:
the face of God gone sour
at an apple bite—
our technological touch
that heals Hippocrates
and staunches the sliced heart
of the dying Indian chief.
All the glory of the stars
melt down the dark blue sky
and the red stripes congeal
on the wounded soldier's cheek.

Creeks of our Badlands overflow
with massacred ponies;
their naked riders, feathered dust
in the prairie winds.
Red and white stripes—

women and children forming
the bony substructure
of our Midwestern farms.

Ready for the Undertaker?

The college presidents who skate
on the thin schizophrenic ice
that skims the depths
of their copulating minds
brood over the distance
maintained against them
between their shadows and the Shadow;
their symbols and their selves.
They have let down their hair
as sackcloth, a curtain
hiding empty eyes
determining change.

Ready for the Undertaker?

And the braided professors,
Latinate, learned, languid
in professing the Liberal Arts
twisting the language of love
to pretzel their heartsview,
imagine their scribbles to be
tomorrow's lasting monuments.
Milton, be glad of your blindness,
and Blake, of your innocent stance.
They serve to disguise
their artistic designs
in all that they know:
Et in Arcadia ego

The Blue Boy, the boy-next-door,
velvet, unframed,
steps out of the picture,

flung from the conjugal nest,
rests his silver shield
on the verge of his tongue.
He has become, at our behest,
a great legal revolver,
spinning the compass,
pressing the compress
against us.

He is always ready to shoot
through the masks of our dreams:
smashed smile, twisted ear,
the slippery viscera sliding
three thousand miles
out of the botched belly
of the American Dream.

His middle-aged wife,
bathed in her creams:
anodynes to erase the lines
of death from her husband's face;
her idle-aged husband, destined
to travel, unlubricated,
ten point five miles
through her dark Fallopian tubes,
to work his destination by daybreak:
the bawdy birth of a Fata Morgana—
the world crunched up in a seed
passed between the lips of Adam and Eve:
something born into nothing again.

Ready for the Undertaker?

The children, our children,
angels lapping up time
between now and then;
they pursue God in the labels
at the Five-and-Ten

while He survives them
with omnipotent leaps,
in spite of timetables.
He is the arriving train
and the departing plane,
always coming or going
but never on time,
never at the right time.
Late while they wait;
early, leaving them surly
at the wrong gate—
God! thundering off for appointments
and never making them
here in America.

And, though they never arrive,
our children may make it,
trickling smokes of glory
and sunbursts of stone,
skidding into heaven
on a mushroom cap.

Yes, our Children Tyrannos,
who eat up our bodies
and suck out our bones
until we feel the country's pelvis
dissolve in an ulcerous, digestive groan.

Ready for the Undertaker?

So, swallow this lump. Dump
the pulped bodies of pickers—
Spick, spate, Spock—
to fertilize the wet lettuce
of California fields.
We garden the businessman
who uses their grease
for the nuts and bolts
of his skeletal hand;

his right hand fingers our goods;
his left hand fingers us good.

Man, God, and the American dollar:
God and the American dollar
conceive of man behind the IBM machines;
Man and the American dollar
conceive of God behind the altarcloths;
the Catholic priest and the laity,
the Episcopal bishop and the choir soprano
conceive of the American dollar
behind the last, dark pew.

Ready for the Undertaker?

The civil American Right
enjoys its right to ride
down the eyes of Mississippi,
the large, lacey eyes
of "dem pickaninnies,"
harvesting the cotton swabs
of Southern morticians.
Their colored mothers support a race
of lunatics with the tips
of their nipples. the thrust
of their thighs in the long, red hours
that fill up our nights,
buttock-wet and tongue-tied
in Gethsemane's gardens.

So, the Negroes, oh God, yes!
the Negroes again, and the Jews:
bandied bait of New Nazis—
Nig Jigg, spite, Kike:
quantitative democracy blooming
in the dawn of a new night;
quota equality, more equal than equal,
greening America in the valley of love,

stuffing up the noses of angels—
all pro one nation and anti the rest,
making the nation safe, making the nest
downy with hatsful of hate.

And the white lovelything,
a new bride of matched fortune,
swinging her husband into the thighs
of the charming, old bitch down the street,
lifts up her pure veil, revealing her vineyard—
grapes, free for the plucking;
red wine in the making,
all yours for the taking
any day of the week.

Oh Christ! what a howl of love
coils Chicago's Loop,
juices New Orleans' jazz
and Pisas the Empire State Building
with tremors that drain
light out of the City's dawn.

Ready for the Undertaker?

The domed city, the new Benares
burning on the Potomac bank,
buys our Harvard lawyers,
our Yale Phd's
our Irish millionaires,
and our Texas ranchers,
readies itself for new death marches,
greases up the Washington Monument
with the assorted lard of liberals,
the hipped and the gypped,
smokers, mainliners. stoned cats,
Holy Ghosters, co-ed cadres,
the gee and haw
of the faked-out, freaked-out

evangelical outriders
of the American Apocalypse.

And, above us all, her nose in the clouds,
her spiked hat scraping the sky's bottom,
massaging heaven and the rump of God,
the stony-faced, stony-heart
Lady of the Harbor, detached from the Main,
standing in solitude, in the sun and the rain,
islanded, her torch stuck in the country's eye,
cannot even speak the country's language
and listens to faulty translations
of Eighteenth Century French.
She cannot be breached on her beach
by the spear of our love.
Her ossified ovaries cannot produce
New Sons of Liberty.

Ready for the Undertaker?

THE WILL THAT IN THE SUNSET
FINDS RELEASE

The Will that in the sunset finds release
finds my eyes cold
and fills them with new light;

that drives the bee to flower
drives me,
and I can never be
both honeyed flower and bee;

that drives the wind to trees
tries me,
and I can never be
both wind and budded tree;

that drives the flower to seed
seeds me,
and I can never taste
the honey with the bee.

The Will that in the flower grows to soul
finds my soul cold
and fills it with new breath;

that breathes new green in grass
greens me,
and I can never tell
the flower from the bee;

that moves the seed to bloom
blooms me,
and I can never will
the flower not to be.

The Will that moves the bloom to blow
blows me,
and I can never grow
to soul, to flower, to bee.

A DIRGE FOR THE DEAD ANATOLY

for Tony Swerbinsky, runner

You lie there lonely and alone
in the cushioned coffin case,
your dark serge suit against
the satin's white bouffant.

Even close up you seem
a distant portrait now,
hazy, indistinct,
heavy with ultimate gravity.

I want to shout into your ear:
Get up! Throw them the lie
of the mortician's careful part
in this dumbshow of barbaric art.

Who blesses and redeems dead Anatoly
in your deep Ukrainian sleep?
Who kisses your cold careful face
with memories of living love?

Ah, Tony, this is no place
for either you or me—
the acting school of cold eternity.
I know that I can rise and leave;

but you must stay and must endure
this stiff and silent legacy,
Death's artful piece,
while all your litheness
cries for imminent release.

Let's run together, then; race
at least in metaphor, away
from this dull, exacting place
into the sunlight burning bright
in the living August day.

HOTHOUSE

In the still heat—
the fierce silence of sun
beating without thunder
on the hothouse glass—
the windless, cloudless world
where love grows exotic,
winds through green stems.
bursts finally, quietly,
into flaming bloom
blazing through panes,
until the hothouse burns
with the passion
of atoms unchained,
in slow, delicious motion.

A BIRD IN WINTER

I was near to dreaming when the bird came,
sat still and silent in the bushtips
on the outskirts of my winter sleep.

I'd say it is demanding landscape there
between the world and winter dream
where every rut and rill exhorts
exact attention from the will.
The bird seemed frozen to the ground.

Snow lay soft as down upon its feathered back;
its shadow, black, softer than silence,
contradicted every rut and rill.

It was a wild thing, longing for spring
that sat in silence in the deepening snow
without an eye-move to mark the spot,
seeming to take winter into itself.

Something that was me yet left outside,
shivered in worn feathers for the warm treetop,
searched for rest and found itself
inside that quivering breast.

Though I was restless against the weight of sleep
and tossed against the greater weight of March,
the colder weather inside found
a meeting place with winter
in the silent flutter of a sleeping bird.

UPSTATE MARCH

Helmeted sky! the country's
chained in snow.

No one else is here to hear
the sure boneclick of twigs
snapped in the iron air.

Once in a buried time,
you and I
made one design of contrast
with this wintry tale:
close shadows closing
on the snow,
bold, black prints
that followed
where the pale sun
would go.

Now, the day shivers in armor:
above, the sky clangs
as the visor drops,
shutting out daylight.

Trees stalk the stars,
sharp birches
blending with snow;
branches bare as arms,
trunks split like thighs
in the wide moonlight.

The wind whets the tongue
to a pointed cry,
It is still "I love you,"
but the sound clicks
like the snap of bone and twig.

VISITING THE CAGES IN BOMBAY
India, 1970

At the Grand Hotel in Bombay,
we were told
we could visit the Cages
in an Indian cab
with a displaced Punjabi
driving, stiff
in his turned-up toes.

The house fronts were grilled,
barred up like cages,
not for us to peek through,
which we did, observing
the nightly maneuvers of love
sold by the rupee,
but for the women to see
at a knock, judging the men.

Life in the Cages is sweet
as the brush of a crow's wing
over the dead face of a Sikh.

A woman with her heart
bright in her almond eyes
bared her breasts for the Sahibs;
rupees burned on her tongue
as she softly called out
in moist Hindustani;
and, not knowing the language,
we understood what she said.

Love in the Cages is sweet
as the incense of dung
rising up from the street.

Later, over tea by the fire,
I rubbed my mind raw
on the grate of desire,

seeing India rise in the steam
of the boiling pot of Bombay,
shackled in centuries of women
selling their hands and their feet;
and I thought for a moment
of my past Army days,
of a bare-breasted Negress
asleep in her slat-shaded room
somewhere on North Deerborn Street.

IN THE MADRAS MARKET
India, 1995

In the Madras market, a woman
offers me flowers
with her hands and her eyes:

jasmine and hibiscus
are the odor of god
in a profusion of light.

I am overwhelmed
with the passion of jasmine,
the flame of hibiscus,
the brilliance of god.

Everywhere small suns
explode in the market—
flowers send forth love
in a fragrant code
that only women can know.

Ragas of love rage in the air
to the strings of sitar,
to the tap of tabor,
to the faint froth of flute:
voices of god everywhere.

But I have been smothered
by jasmine,
burned by hibiscus,
blinded by god
with his burnished eye.

So love escapes me,
and the market flows on
in a flooding of music,
in a flooding of light,
in a flooding of flowers,
burning bright with god's light.

THE HIGHWAY TO DELHI

This road is a ribbon that runs
from Agra to Delhi,
and the ribbon is twisted and tied.
We are alive.

Busses and trucks vie
for a spot on the road.
They skim their sides,
but Ganesh, Remover of Problems,
presides.

I can hear his trumpet blast
in the dust-filled air;
it rings in the ear. He is a heavy tusker who cares.

Now, it is easier to pass
through a camel's eye
than to pass
on the highway to Delhi.

The traffic pattern
is jam all the way,
and the day
is streaked with its stain.

Scooters fly off to the sky;
shadowless walkers rush by.
Each image explodes in the eye,
magnified,
in the violet panes of the bus
as the oncoming traffic drowns us.

Horns sound animal cries
in the dust and the dung
as our lungs
burst with the heat.

We are one with the road
as we load
mile upon mile toward Delhi.

Sharada just smiles and smiles.
She knows there is nought she can do.
But odd Ramaswamy is ohming,
hoping that Krishna will too,

We all try to move to the rear,
but I know
there is nothing to fear:
our driver's expert at the wheel
with sinews of steel
and nerves compounded
of sunlight and stone.

He is alone in ecstatic delight
as he winds his wheel
with celestial light.

Is he the Cosmic Dancer?
There is no definitive answer,
but lightning is not faster
than his skill at the wheel.

We miss trucks by a hair,
busses by the width
of a finger
cut off at the joint.

We jump and we jolt.
The bus rears up and bolts
down the road
from Agra to Delhi.

It is karma *a la mode*,
and Nirvana,
just around a corner or two.

WAITING FOR THE THIRD WAVE IN

Out on the hot Pacific,
out on the unknown waters,
with the cruiser listing
after the kamikazes
like dragon tongues
had licked her guntubs,
scorching steel,
melting it down to the water,
but the planes now downed;
her long rifles, stretched skyward,
drawn and thin like dumb fingers
searching the skies
for heavenly winds;
the sailors drop down,
torn like sails by shot;
they fall down ladders,
through bulkheads,
down the sides and the hatches,
dying on decks.
Shore parties have landed,
stranded now on the beaches;
marines mangled on reefs,
wrenched on the bridgeheads,
raining on islands.

We stand in the fantail,
watching the shore,
the jungle on fire,
palm trees flying,
the sand beach sprinkled with dead,
the Japanese soldiers retreating
into the jungle
as wasps roll up in mud balls,
the whole atoll burning.

And, we lean downwind,
yearning for islands, waiting
the bo's'n's pipe

and the returning craft
for the third wave in;
watching the frogmen leap,
stringing their streamers
from ship to shore,
dyes red in the water,
guidelines to slaughter.
And, off to the west,
sun down
bleeding
over the island.

TO A KOREAN COMFORT GIRL
SHOT SNIPING

I called to her in loving, deadly voice,
the comfort girl behind the hiding bush;
she turned, and I sent home the bolt
to kiss a bullet to her waiting heart.
How could I know that tears
could water foes,
who never knew that women fought
in wars that cracked men's souls.

After a firefight on hills
July-fierce in May,
snipers caressing us;
the blunted bullets whining,
ricocheted from rocks, biting
the afternoon to death,
I shot the loving sniper.

Crouched upon rocks,
hidden in branches
of shelled, uprooted trees,
she capsulated death.
When her dark hair grew long
without her cap, I knew
and felt the fishbone choke;
volley of sorrows gunning through
like lightning shooting beyond truth:

there, on a hill in May,
hot, under a July sun,
my rifle melted, drops
like dew under the sun;
her sweet, rich smell
passing, a whiff of love
caught with blood and sun.

I FIND THE DEAD CHINAMAN

The day shouts
with pain
as the guns resume again:
shell after shell hurled
until the eyelids curl
with fat fatigue.
The whole world in league
with war:
the napalm burning,
the sky turning
red with rockets
burning holes
in the parchment blue.

I turn then to you,
the one dead
instead of me,
ashing slowly,
pulsating
in the heavy sun,
new to the state of grace,
finding fault
with the fruit
picked from the bush
below which you lie,
a graceful line of light
shining through
the gray and ashy form
that fathoms now
the plentitude
that once was you.

In the flow of death
surrounding me,
I see
the instant
of your fierce desire.

You swallowed fire
and took it with you
to the fertile ground;
when all around
were breathing air
you grew volumes
in the dusty smoke.

Each jellied stroke
that smote your face,
your hands, your heart,
placed you apart
from blood and flesh.
You looked at fire, fresh
from the start
as an ikon
worshipped
in head and heart.

You lie before me,
spare and clean,
purged of body,
pure and lean,
marking the place
where you and I,
meeting, have made one
where one must live,
and one must die.

EASTER, 1951

Once in the hard heart of the mountains
on an Easter Sunday
where we were a thin line
with the shell-shocked pines,
waiting for the chaplain to come
for a Christ-rising service
in the rain and mud of the mountains,
waiting with the empty cans we had to bury,
never knowing why, except
some sergeant said we should,
suspecting the gleam, the shine sinister,
spreading like the broken pines
in the falling rain,
spreading like the line of men;
and someone said, perhaps,
MacArthur might inspect the lines.

There, after the firefights had stopped,
after the night had ended in rain,
after the planes had all gone
deep into the weather,
after the thin rain had softened again,
had put out the napalm, the fires;

there, after the fires smoked,
after the broken trees, the pines, smoked
and stood still in the rain
like the black bodies of the nurses stood,
burned in the jeeps of the wrecked column,
smoking on Easter Sunday;
there, where we passed the charred hand
of the Chinese soldier,
crisped by the phosphorous,
right in the middle
of the Chinese Fourth Field Army,
and saw the burned arm smoking
with light leaking out
between the lines of ash and rain;

there, where the South Korean generals
were caught hiding out
and shot for refusing to fight;
where the Allied soldiers fought,
died in the drenched trenches
and emptied out into Easter
like logs into sloshy valleys,
into the rice paddies,
into the soggy generals
crumpled before village walls,
into the charred Chinese hand,
into the burned nurses, the broken pines,
into the empty cans, past where we ran
out of the heart of the mountains
on Easter Sunday, ran past the log jam,
the log-packed valleys, and past a new thing
in the thin line of men and rain;
a French soldier, someone said,
but all that we could see
was a man jack-knifed in a hole,
buried, head down in the dirt,
ass up in the rain,
planted for all time,
a marker marking time for us
on Easter Sunday;

there, where we ran past the empty cans,
the empty dead, the empty hands, the empty heads,
after the rain had washed out
the heart of the mountain,
washed out their dead,
washed the charred nurses white again,
washed the Chinese hand yellow again,
washed the generals brave again,
washed the French soldier's face clean again,
making Easter a long wet time
in our empty minds
when the chaplain failed to arrive.

when we waited, waited all day
for the nurses to starch fresh again,
for the Chinese hand to salute again,
for the Korean generals to stand up again,
for the French soldier to upright again,
even for the Chinese Fourth Field Army
to come up the hills again
on Easter Sunday;

all, all failing to arrive,
even after we had shaved downstream in the rain
when someone said the chaplain might arrive,
the Chinese might come,
perhaps MacArthur might inspect the lines,
inspect the empty cans, the burned nurses,
inspect the charred hand, the dead generals,
inspect the French soldier and his ass,
inspect the late chaplain,
inspect even the Chinese Fourth Field Army;

and I gagged on the beans from the empty cans,
on the burned nurses, the charred hand,
gagged on the packed logs, the late chaplain,
on the shot generals, the French soldier,
gagged on MacArthur and the whole Chinese Fourth Field Army,
gagged on Easter Sunday; and the war went on and on and
on...

RESCUE BY HELICOPTER

Nosing the sun,
noisy blades glint gossamer
invisible in fast flight,
the chopper rises
banging its burden
in the lateral boxes,
sore bone against good wood--
rises up higher,
the bubble bursting,
splintered with light.

This is how I have seen them
climbing the sun,
biting the bright blue sky,
brilliant dragonflies
bumping their bulge-eye
against the shattering light.

Now I am in darkness,
cocooned
after the shelling,
here in the lateral box,
biting the blood on my lips.

I can hear the slight whir,
buzzing of bullets
zipping the sky;
now and again one thuds
dull, striking the wood,
shaking the pine dust.

Everything rushes:
the chopper rises;
small splinters of sun
split the dark:
light chews wood.

Below me, the contending men
shoulder the darkness,
bear up the leaving night
on their humped backs
while we rise up,
one with the climbing sun.

CHEESE

They had set the cheese down
between them on the floor
after they arrived,
my friends from Wisconsin,
and it swelled up until
the whole room existed
for the sake of the cheese.

Their minds were perforated—
dotted with holes of memory gone,
the war evacuated.
But, after admiring the cheese,
the holes filled up and we
talked blue streaks
about the living and the dead;
the holes in which we lived,
empty, too, of memory and of us;
the infinite dots of time,
scattered between gunshots,
that we'd filled up with longing
for Wisconsin cheese.

Theirs had been a repartee
of cheese—cheddar and Swiss—
remitting the long hours
between fights.
I had been the cupped ear
for their musings,
until I, too, thought Paradise
in giant curds.

Death stopped once, moved on,
and turned a corner of the war.
We saw his arms filled
with dairy boys as he churned
the burning hills beyond the sun.

Now, we talk cheese and wait,
impatient for the eating.

THE BLUE SKY MOTEL
1952

Here I am
in the rugged room
of the motel
I have yearned for
during the monsoon months
under the wet canvas
in the pine woods
on the big mountains;
the room with the rugged floor
and the rugged walls
and the ceiling done
in soft orange
floral design
with red pomegranates
growing in green leaves.

I have told myself
that after the war was over
I would grow up,
I would settle down,
I would, perhaps, even marry.

And now I am here
in the Blue Sky Motel,
waiting for her to finish
her washroom obligations,
and she isn't the redhead
I thought she would be,
the one with the svelte skin,
the long, thin legs and swivel hips
dreamed together in impossible angles
under the wet canvas
in the mountain woods;
but some other woman,
larger than I thought
a woman could be
under all that loose dress.
I shall eat an old honeycomb

and suck it dry
as she comes to me
with fire in her groin
and spittle in her eye.

After the war was over,
I had said
I would settle down,
I would grow up,
go down, perhaps, even marry.

She comes to me large and hairy.
Her legs heavy with walking,
paunchy, and more aware
of her drooping breasts
swaying with her walk
across the red rugged floor
than I of the staggering fact
of the soft, rugged walls molding,
of the pomegranates falling
from the overripe ceiling,
of the rank garden smells,
and the tarnished weeds,
bleeding blue milk.

What with the war over
and the monsoon done
and the wet canvas forgotten
and the mountains standing still
in the Asian sunlight
twenty thousand miles away
and the long parade of women
that spilled out of naked minds
ending at last
in the red rugged room
of this blue motel,
I say to myself
that I will grow up,
I will settle down,
I will, perhaps, even marry.

A DEAD HORSE IN THE SUPERMARKET

The horse was dead center
in my mind,
and my mind reeked
with its indecency:
belly blown open wide,
demonstrating
the indelible construction
with miles of entrails,
pink and smoking
in the winter air.

Here, I am slipping fast
into middle age,
lost for days
in the supermarket,
investigating the comedy
of meat:
slick steaks cut fresh
from the cold-blooded sides;
the pulsating polyp of liver
in its bloody bath;
the interminable long links
of sausage,
pink and slippery
in the cool case.

But, I think of the horse,
obviously, again and again,
seeing its awkward architecture
made yet more awkward,
even grotesque,
by bombardment:
the horse on its back,
its legs frozen stakes
in the blue air;
its large eyes open,
unblinking, as glassy
as the eyes of large fish
hanging from steel hooks
in the cool case;

the steaming
from the cooling blood
frosting the blue air,
frosting the glass
of the cool case.

I think of the horse
killed by cannon;
what is it to me
now at fifty,
wincing my way
through the supermarket,
gathering
all the useless data
of cuts and weights,
tenderness and color,
as if in some incredible way
everything essential in me
depends on it?

The horse had frozen fast
to the rutty road;
we passed it quickly,
not so much revulsed
by its condition
as by the senseless need
for its wintry death—
marines marching to the line
where death waited
in padded jacket and pile cap
with bullet and bayonet
to rip our entrails out,
to turn the fresh snow
to red slush
before nightfall.

I have problems in the market
finding my way
past the cool cases
piled with red meat.

My wife doesn't understand
my reluctance to leave,
my need to linger,
to finger
the variety of meats.
She claims it is
some finer sensuality,
some need of the poet in me
to mingle food with love.
But, then, she doesn't understand
about horses either.

PIECE DE RESISTANCE
for Rex Criminale

That he had fallen through,
that he had strayed
along the way,
lapping libations,
finding relations
between the eating habits
of the rich and poor,
testified to his ardor
in pursuing his amour.
The question left
was only one of truth:
a certain inflation
between
the tongue and tooth.

He was, we note,
a late-comer
to the door of love—
which, too, must be defined—
having spent time
on the make
from the age of nine
when he observed,
through an open kitchen door,
the virtues of a *Soup de Jour.*

He vowed that the *Souffle*
would be a doormat
to his worship-house,
both bell and temple,
candle, priest and host.

After that,
it was a simple joust
with roasts and breads
and *Crepes Suzette,*
until he learned

the sinful nature
of French cooking
could outweigh
domestic cares
by several hairs.

Finally,
it was in the latitude,
in the freedom
and the spasm of space
that he allotted in the time
between the pan
and stirring hand
that held him
paramour to passion.

The Spanish omelette,
with pomp and opulence,
became his calling card.

Thereafter,
charge or no,
Lepanto
recurred at will:
his lances broke
beneath the throw
of artichoke
stuffed with white grape,
of firm red snapper filled
with delicate crab
as fine as Spanish lace
and the incredulous mix
of passion with anchovy.

In a word,
his culinary touch
became too much

for his mortal essence
to endure.

It was in the mystic mood
produced by capered veal
sautéed in sweet vermouth,
that in a single bound
up from the cooking ground
of his mortality,
he triumphed
over flesh and blood,
became immortalized
in Spain and France
and found himself,
among the gods,
his own *piece de resistance.*

LADY WITH A SMALL DOG

She ambles amiably along
the tree-lined street
in the center of Xi'an—
small town of a mere
two million plus
an equity of bikes—
and she is preceded by
a small lap dog,
tender, tan and white,
tethered on a leather leash.

She is much too large to be
Han Chinese,
run of the Chinese mill—
more likely a Mongolian lady,
abundant, nonchalant,
or Mandarin-speaking Manchu,
rather shady.

She has consorted with the cadres,
we are told by Mr. Wu
who knows about these things,
consorted and cavorted, too.
Hence, the small lap dog
led by leash in hand
in this hungry land
where Shao Shi Peng has said,
"We eat everything bred
that has four legs,
except a table,
and we would eat that too
if we were able."

We feel some principal
principle has died
in the bare fact that we see
a lap dog here at all
in the petless P.R.C.

She speaks, and the trees
lining the boulevard part;
the summer breeze starts
to eat away the charcoal haze
that filters Xi'an summer days.

More curious than amazed,
we ask Wu
what is that the lady
speaks with such passion vocalized.

He says we must not be surprised
by Mrs. Chong's request:
she would like to have us buy
her pretty dog to pet
or to supply us with some sort
of Chinese shepherd's pie.

We are properly horrified
and say so without delay,
whereupon the languid lady winks and drones
in slow and breathy moans
that have the portent
of Confucian Odes.

Poor Wu grows faint and groans.
There is more in his tone
that forebodes
things more dangerous
than can be found
in old Confucian Odes.

We ask, of course.
that he translate both wink and mood;
yet that he tailor his reply
in an English not so crude
as that Chinese shepherd's pie.

He says the lady asks
if we do not wish to buy
her sweet lap cur,
would we, perhaps, consider
buying her?

LUNCH AT THE CHINESE NATIONAL ART INSTITUTE

We eat the humidity and heat
in the airless room
and slick down our sticking clothes:
the beer warm;
the food cold;
the grease congealed upon our plates;
the windows broken and so smeared
with alluvial dirt that no sun
dare shine through.

It's Ming Dynasty dirt, I tell you—
the real thing—
drowning down from Manchurian clouds
as big as all get-out,
just south of Beijing.

But the green-eyed flies
find the way clear
through broken glass
for ferocious assaults
on the rice pot,
sticky with its own starch glue,
its sides a mélange
of ricey rivulets, sliding
silently and sad
to the welcoming boards
of the littered floor.

We eat ravenously
like Mongolian hordes
deprived of sustenance
since Kubla Khan
mounted the Heavenly Throne;

and the droning wings and buzz
of dysentery settle down
upon our plates

as we wait
for winter melon soup,
and our stomachs do the loop-de-loop,
and the old woman with the her hair strung down
comes round with her pail of rags
to sop the rice up from the floor,
preparing for tomorrow's *Soup de Jour.*

SHAO SHI PENG SPEAKS TOILETS

"Toilets are not," I am told
with Peng's patriotic fervor,
"a Chinese passion."

"We have more to accomplish
with passion
than do the barbarians," says Shao.

I would say that passion
is at best a digression
or hyperbole in this case.

The truth, closer to unconcern,
a naughty neglect, or a certain
distaste of sanitation—
a working out of the Chinese rural mind
in an urban world.

The raw sewage in the streets
of Xi'an speaks passion.

The beautiful Chinese girl
in mini-skirt and high heels
with wondrous fishnet
stockings, standing
at the edge
of that swirling pool
in the Xi'an street,
speaks passion.

The long, dead rat,
black, with its own red blood
creating an expressive art,
lying on the pavement
between two hungry men
and waiting to go home
with them for supper,
now that speaks passion;
now that is a rhetoric

that cannot be resolved
with patriotic fervor.

Shao Shi Peng smiles
and speaks toilets
in the air-conditioned room.
Passion is flushed down the drain.

MR. GUPTA, MR. LI

In the narrow coach
of the Suzhou train
where the air congeals
from the heat
and the sunrise strikes
the window panes
out of the Chinese east,
Mr. Gupta in suit and tie
eats curry with his fingers
while on the next hard seat
across the aisle,
Mr. Li's gaze
from his one good eye
lingers on Gupta's Cola bottle;
and I pretend not to see
the sly theft
of Li's eye
as it steals from the bottle
to the curry piled high,
but how my mind devours
such inequity
as Li's good eye
eats the rich curry..

Ah, Mr. Gupta, fat and mean.
Ah, Mr. Li, hungry and lean.

EVERYONE LOVED FALA

Everyone loved Fala,
even the hungry men
fainting in breadlines.

And, when the Blue Eagle
turned into a brass-clawed Harpy
and the industrial cog clogged
and the strikers at Republic Steel
shot it out with the guards,
Fala was still lovable.

She was always National News,
even when my mother,
filled with unwise love,
got those goddamn khaki knickers
from Relief, along with spicy oranges;
and I whisked, whisked, whisked
down the long hall from 3rd Grade
with my head in my hands
covered with a black cloth.

And, we could hear her barking
nightly from the White House lawn
when at 6 o'clock we sat down to eat,
cutting an orange three ways.

Everyone loved Fala.

HER ROOM AT NIGHT

Her room at night
is a warm, womanly nest;
and she is full,
bursting in black.

How have I touched,
without sight,
her body cocooned
in darkness,
each stroke soft
but bursting light.

What birds fly there!
Enormous colors now and then
and then the dark again.

And I have grasped
at peacock tails
festooned upon the walls,
caught at red parrots
parading there.

And the ceiling lit
with the half-light
of dawn
and the piping of birds
wakes me to sleep.

THE UNIVERSE OF DEATH
for Sylvia Plath

Sylvia in the oven:
her body a cough
and a scrawl in crouch;
and the blue gas,
cool and delicious,
hissing in her ear's soft shell.

Did she think of rescue then:
the charging knight who rode her
breaking the door down
at the penultimate moment
to carry her off
beyond the natural world,
away from the sticky fingers
of blackberries, the claws
of thistle and flower,
the sick honey of bees?

Did she feel the light transport
of her spirit, edging
from the hooked body, verging,
ready for flight?
Did she desire death
to come like this—
sibilant and slow
in the blue gas curls
caressing her breasts,
kissing her mouth a ruby red?
Was it just a sensual fling
that aroused her to the oven?

Or, did despair, at last,
catch her off guard,
she who had lain so long
in the dark cellar hole
with the belljar hung close,
keeping life outside;

she who had safely fed
the two children,
made up the bed,
locked the door,
stuffed the cracks and crevices
of windows with old rags,
and then without prayer,
probably without some comment
resting on her closing heart,
turned on the gas?

She had known despair enough
for it to be an intimate.
Hardly off guard, then—
more likely open-eyed,
welcoming despair
like a Sunday visitor
come to tea
on an English afternoon.

Whatever it was that clouded her,
that caught her finally in those hours
after the fire of Ariel had consumed
most of what remained within
her wondrous circle of heart and mind,
let it rest with her
whose spirit, never resting,
does not rest now,
but brands and torches minds
that travel through her poems
and races onward, spurred,
without bee sting or blackberry nettle
to mix her with the universe of death.

A FABLE OF FLIES

In the western twilight sky
where the sunset glows,
a Great Spirit rose
and said,
"God, I'm bored!
I need something to try,
some thing new. Lord,
I know what I know and am what I am." And so,
he spread out his hands
and said:
"Let there be light
over the whole con-ti-nent,
America, I mean.
I've done the rest.
Let this light be the best."
And there was light,
nice and bright.

And then, the Great Spirit said, "Ah-men:
Ah! Men. Let there be men.
Let there be Redmen."
And there were Redmen aplenty,
but not too many.
And he said: "Let there be deer
and antelope, too. Let them play
where the skies are not cloudy all day."
And they did.
And the Great Spirit said:
"Give them a home and let buffalo roam."
And the buffalo roamed and roamed and roamed.
And all this went on for some time
and bye n' bye,
the Great Spirit roared:
"I'm bored. Great Lord!
there are too many buffalo roaming,
too many antelope playing,
too many deer,
scattered here, scattered there.
Too many kinds of Redmen.

It's been a bad plan.
All in all, Redman, antelope, buffalo
and nothing else to show."

So, he played around with making a moon
and some stars.
And he invented 12 o'clock noon
and the Spanish guitar,
and, then, he got himself an idea balloon
to help change his plan.
And the Great Spirit finally said:
"Let there be the white man.
That'll put a change in the plan.
Let him have pie in the sky.
Let him be fruitful! Let him multiply.
And he did. Why he multiplied like flies.
And soon there were Italian flies
and Spanish flies,
Dutch flies and English flies,
and even the French fly.
And they multiplied and they multiplied
until some of those flies got the notion
to fly over the At-lan-tic Ocean.
And they did.

And after a while, they multiplied in style,
and there were New York flies and New Jersey flies,
New Hampshire flies and Connecticut flies,
and even Philadelphia and Levittown flies.
And the Great Spirit cried:
"I've had enough of these flies."
But they multiplied and they multiplied,
and before he knew it, he knew he blew it.
So, there were Michigan flies and Wisconsin flies,
Independence, Missouri flies,
and even a few Iowa flies.

And the Great Spirit said that he couldn't top it.
And when he said that he couldn't stop it,
he certainly was truthful,
'cause the magic word was... fruitful !
And though he tried and tried,
they multiplied and they multiplied
until there were river flies and mountain flies,
desert flies and prairie flies,
and even a George Armstrong Custer fly.

And the Great Spirit said:
"Good Lord! What a nasty horde!
But I'll have my way, the final say.
I always do, ain't it true?"
And, so, The Great Spirit worked.
He labored six days and he labored six nights,
and as things got hotter and hotter,
on the seventh day he invented
the first fly swatter.

And he swatted them left
and he swatted them right
and he swatted them day
and he swatted them night
and he really tried,
but those flies were real fruitful,
and they multiplied and they multiplied,
and the Great Spirit said:
"Those flies are on a roll.
Why Great God, they outta control."
And they were. And finally those flies flew
across the whole nation,
and the Great Spirit said:
"God knows I tried,
but I need a vacation."
And he did. And those flies?
Why, they multiplied and they multiplied.

Then, the flies in a mighty fine fit
bit and bit.
And who was around to bite? Right!
Why, the Redman, of course.
They bit him on the hills
and they bit him on the plains,
bit him awake and bit him sleepy,
and they bit him right outta his own tepee,
until finally in one giant bite
the Redman fell right outta sight:
the Sioux and the Ute and the Na-va-ho,
the Apache, the Piute and A-rap-a-ho,
and with them the buffalo, the buffalo,
and the deer and the antelope too.

And, after the biting and after the cries,
after the treaties and after the lies,
why all that were left were the flies.
And they multiplied
and they multiplied
and they mul-ti-plied.

M. DEL PAPA

M. Del Papa, friend to man,
who lined his pockets
with his countrymen,
fondled New World riches in his hand
and ordered a poor man's paradise be found
before some latter day Prometheus,
finding fire, be unbound
to satisfy his countrymen's desires.

Often have I stood
as boy and man
before his mausoleum, grand
edifice to his mortality
and wondered just how he
could truly be
such glorious friend to man.
I saw the grand materialism
of his open hand
extended out to everyone
in M. Del Papa Land.

A penny lying underneath
a railroad tie became
a synonym
for M. Del Papa's name;
a lesson in procurement
of great personal wealth;
a way to riches and long health;
and so the young men learned
who lifted heavy ties
until they found the penny,
still Sibyl bright,
exactly where it fell,
a moment lingering astray
this side of hell
as payment for Del Papa's way,
when it came time for him to die:
a cover for a Roman eye.

And they cried, "Have you
urged us to remove
this pile of monumental ties
for the sake of a single penny bright?"

His answer stunned them with delight
with its logical insight:
"How did I become
a Croesus in this land
if not by saving every cent at hand?"

And in the years that I grew up
my father swore by this:
Del Papa could not be remiss.
Yet, every cent that came our way
was spent to keep the wolf away,
and M. Del Papa's sage advice
thought of more than once or twice,
was most impractical if nice;
and while we lived as poor as mice,
M. Del Papa gained a slice
of the rich man's Paradise.

.

MY RICH CROATIAN UNCLE, ANDY SMITH

Memory be a brazen route
running to the richness
of my Croatian uncle,
Andrus von der Rosenblatt—
heavy Germanic name draped
over his narrow Slavic shoulders
to remind him of the blood
mixed in his narrow veins
and the rooted pain
as he moved from Balkan town
to repetitious Balkan town
until he came
to a new name in this strange American place—
born anew instantly
in 1932:
the court adjudged,
the judge approved:
Andy Smith, American—
innocuous and unoffending
to the public eye,
except, perhaps, for his bad temper
and bad tongue,
the strange, hard accents lingering,
seemingly harmless, really,
over the crude English words;
except, perhaps, too, for his swearing
in sounds guttural and cruel;
and for the heavy stomp
of his left lame foot
in pounding out the polkas
and mazurkas
at the Catholic church bazaars
or at my grandfather's birthday feasts,
those ominous occasions which,
despite their outward gaiety and charm,
gave forth the direst alarms
and threatened the uneasy peace
of New Year Eves—

birthdays of portentous signs
and overemphasizing omens of ill will
for all the brothers-in-law
and dutiful daughters of the grandfather,
the gorgeous grandfather
of calamitous disturbances,
displays of sheer disgrace
and catastrophic threats
of rank and massive mayhem,
straddling the midnight hour
in the high glee galas
of his birthday prowess.

Yes, that same Andy Smith, American,
once buried alive in a drainage ditch,
dug out by hand of a great black man—
the left leg forever lamed—
friend for life, friend for a day;
that Andy Smith,
as prone to violence as a dagger
poised when the whiskey hit him
in just the right way,
stimulated,
encouraged senselessly,
set up by the grandfather antics
into panics of prodigious pain,
his square, narrow head
swelling through blood-streaked eyes,
such small gray-green eyes
filled with Balkan fever;
but he would cross into his crass Croatian
at the barest hint of reprimand—
the uncle, childless,
but rich with a heavy wife,
the beautiful Belinda of dreams,
won only after the implacable father,
the grandfather, insisted that he learn
the latter language of Roman legions

to woo and win the maiden
of his Croatian dreams.

So, then, the hard Croatian tones
scratchy, craggy,
touched now with soft scent
of 19th Century Neapolitan Italian,
asked for the hand and body
of Belinda the beloved,
and heated in awesome argument
with the other husbands
of her five sisters,
all Italian in language,
in augmented and essential nature,
my own father among them—
true superman of all my childhood dreams,
gone now to distant Krypton,
crayoned in my child mind
in tones of white and gold.

Gone now, gone all—
to some undoubted place
to where all memories go;
Croatian and Italian,
uncles and soft aunts,
the beautiful Belinda,
my father, superman,
the terrible, loving grandfather
of inexplicable rage,
and all the immense vortex
of that timeless time and place
of my rich Croatian uncle—Andy Smith.
All, all stumble and fall
into that chaotic love
of childhood dreams.

THE SCHOOL NEWSPAPER PHOTOGRAPHER
TAKES SOME SHOTS FOR AN ARTICLE
CALLED "FACULTY FOCUS"

Will you focus your eyes
on the hole, please?
Will you? Will you
not roll them, please?
Will you?

I try not to wheeze.
I check my tight tie
and take it right off,
straighten the skinfolds
and know

how tender skin feels
shaved, scraped
from the face, peeled
in the morning daze.

On my shelves
notebooks yellow
and book bindings break;
hair falls and falls
on the floor,
layer on layer,
useless and gray,
blocking the door,
blocking the way.

Will you glue them together
and use them today?
Will you?
Will you?

I say,
"Meanwhile, there's a studio print
that I like
in your file,

one taken 5 years ago
or so. Can't you use it though?

No! That won't do,
it simply won't do.
We need something new
with a different view.
Will you want one too?
A new one of you?

I say,
"Why not a large lady
with Wagnerian breasts--
breathing beasts
beat by beat,
with only her mountainous chest,
warming the air
in a Brunhilda way;
I'd be out of your hair."

I say,
"Why not a man rather weird
in a second-hand beard,
a man with a Karl Marx glance,
bearing a long, dirty lance
deep in his pants
to bloodpoison plants?
Well, it's worth a chance."

Will you want a copy
for Mother?
One edged in black
for your brother?
One for the album;
another, another?
Will you want one too?
Will you?
Will you?

No need to look at the birdie,
certainly no need
for anything pornographic
or dirty;
and no expression too droll.
Look into the black hole.
It could cut off your head
nice and slick
with one click,
so I'm told.

Will you want a copy
for Father?
A nice 5 by 10
for your daughter?
A copy cut at the throat
to pin on the wall
down the hall?
Will you want any at all?
Will you?
Will you?

I say,
"No need to get riled.
The cut gums reveal
the dentist
who loves me,
the dentist who while
I squirm
drills out the rotten worm
from my smile.

Will you want a copy
for Wife?
A copy bigger than life?
A copy of caries enlarged
for curious colleagues?
Will you want one
for your son,

a shot of your tongue
hanging out on your chin
neat as a pin.

One that could win
some admiration from him?
Will you?
Will you?

After all,
any smile will do,
even a grimace or two,
even a bridge by itself,
completely separate from you.
Will you want a copy or two?
Will you?
Will you?
Will you?

" I do."

DILEMMA

I've been reading evolution theory,
trying to get back
into the primal mud of pond behind the farm.

How hard it is to do
after Adam and the naming of things:
after the tawny lion and the slippery toad,
after the giant Redwood and the warty weed,
after the telescoping of giraffe,
the chipmunk chittering and the lisp
of squirrels sliding the telephone lines,
after the titmouse teetering
on the thinnest branch and the great crow
curving through the sky
in sheer, black-robed telegraphy.

How hard it is to do
after the wonderful fib
of Eve and Adam's rib,
after the infamy of apple,
the notoriety of glitter
surrounding the snake,
the Father filled with wrath,
unforgiving, relentless, but
promising some future fruit.

I'm sure that science is a useful thing,
but how drab and gray it is
beside such metaphors
that ring and sing.

ALL THE LITTLE COMFORTS
Memories of Eichmann and Auschwitz

You had been a most unusual angel
who came in the usual way,
announcing your god.

I think of you often, reluctantly,
resplendently dressed in silver and black,
standing in that strange historical light
that settles down around catastrophe,
a sort of cosmic clerk with your clipboard, counting;
an *isolato* whose breath is a sharp knife in the dark.
You would have served Ahab well.

Some say your pride was boldly creative,
a pride in doing things better than most,
of taking charge of a charge,
discharging it with great detail,
with all the right detail:

a chocolate for a child;
a Strauss waltz for a woman.

I could construe you as a Christ-crushed man
could I view the world as you:
a man of quiet clemency
preparing all the little comforts
for the coming of great Cyclone B:

a chocolate for a child;
a Strauss waltz for a woman.

There have been horses as loyal as you,
horses so loyal, I am told,
that they carried their master in blizzards
until both man and beast
froze in a block of ice..

No one can ever say that you
engaged in that curious activity
of beating a dead horse.

JUMPING OFF THE EIFFEL TOWER
Paris and Berlin, 1972

1.

To look down the windy aisles of the world,
to look toward the huge lump rising
eastward out of the hard Atlantic,
to look where history became
the measure of death;
to finish the job and have done
with all grieving,
with all keening;
with all human crying
in the European graveyard
toward which we have all been heading
this human hundred years,
this Twentieth Century.

Home lies in the West
where the sun goes down
and where darkness waits its turn
to return again,
to creep out on all fours
eastward toward the shores
of Europe
from where love once came,
from where hate once came,
from where the art of life
was fashioned
as the very art of art,
from where the art of death
reached its apex
in the century's dawn.

2..

Vichy water for cleaning
their hands and feet;
mud to squeeze for drinking;

106

cognac for an anesthesia
to the wounded race.

Imagine a god's-eye view:
a million men
practicing the art of dying
around Verdun.
One by one, the French soldiers
dropped into their own Louvres;
one by one, the Germans marched
into Gotterdammerung.

The entire countryside
a museum—
it was as if all Germans
went floating down the Rhine;
as if all France
had lined up in gay Paree
to jump, one by one,
off the Eiffel Tower.

3.

One million men passed
out of sight,
and still the sun was shining,
and still no end in sight.

Today, the lines buried
beneath the earth
point to Verdun,
and the sun strikes a pose
over the horizon
like a searchlight
seeking to point out
an interstice between
heaven and hell.

4.

Each generation we are told
needs its own cleansing,
a washing out of wounds,
a bathing of civilized slights
in the primal rites.

So the bones of the dead
should not rest content
that they will rise again
out of the vast ash pit
by miracle,
but be resurrected premature
by human judgment
documenting eternity:

the sleepers awakened
in the middle of the night,
asked to move out,
asked to leave
to make room for new tenants.
And not only soldiers
coming fresh from fields
with wet wounds,
but a whole new race:
six million unloved men
in a ritual of fire.

How will some god
re-clothe the charred bones
shoveled into lime pits?
or recover the lost bones
now dissolved
into the deep-sprung earth?
or restore the newcomers
late to arrive,
cold and surprised

from living, snuffed out
suddenly by the Russian winter
of all discontent?

5.

Now, we are quiet for the moment,
quiet in these old lands
where April comes each year
with new grass to cover
the old lines pointing still,
ever deeper into the earth
around Verdun.

Europe sleeps in the hands
of the dying century
and waits to wake
in blinding light
of instant resurrection
which will raise up
the living and the dead
into new stars
and new apexes of new sun.

I LOVE YOU, MINNIE WANTAUGH, IN THE A. & P.

I love you, Minnie Wantaugh, in the A. & P.
where you rise up, a vision, pure, pristine,
floating among the melons like some queen
lost out of Egypt; burnished among barges
of yellow squash, enthroned upon the pears—
Bartletts—long and delicious as your breasts.
How gossamer you between the aisles, gliding
on tiny feet around the cans of beets,
bottles of ketchup, mayonnaise, relish
of summer nights upon the Nile, bathed
in Euphrates of olive oil; swinging
from the camel humps of grocery boys,
loading the freezers with tasty creams.
I have seen you, nude, along the sides of beef,
cool and distant under refrigeration,
and have longed for your hot touch
amid the bagels, English muffins,
rye and pumpernickel,
only to swoon at my own daring in seducing
all your virtues near the mushrooms.
Cabbage head! Celery heart! Carrot root!
The sheer saliva slithering at the pearl
tips of scallions ecstasizes me.
I love you, Minnie Wantaugh, and the A. & P.